For my Nan

For my Nan

A Heartwarmers™
Gift Book

For my Nan

A Heartwarmers™ Gift Book

©WPL 2002

Text by Anne Dodds

Additional material by Howard Baker

Illustration by Jo Parry - Advocate

Printed in China

Published by WPL 2002

ISBN 1-904264-09-3

For information on other Heartwarmers™ gift books, gifts and greetings cards, please contact

WPL

14 Victoria Ind. Est. Wales Farm Road

London W3 6UU UK

Tel: +44 (0) 208 993 7268 Fax: +44 (0) 208 993 8041

email: wpl@atlas.co.uk

Nan, this little book is for you
as I wanted to say,
all the things that go unsaid
as life goes on each day.

You are just so special
and I really hope you know,
you'll always mean the world to me
wherever I may go.

My world is just a happier place
knowing that you care,
and when I need someone to talk to
I know you're always there.

You always somehow
make me smile
and the kind things
that you do,
make me feel so very glad
that I have a Nan like you.

Thanks for never judging me
and for trying to understand.
You've never tried to lecture me
just offered a helping hand.

Nan, you've always been looking out
for whatever is best for me.
You're my bridge across the river,
you're my anchor in the sea.

You're my ladder
leading to success,
my safety net if I fall,
and my welcoming committee
whenever I come to call.

From my earliest memories
your smiling face was there,
and I've never ever doubted
just how much you care.

You've laughed with me
and dried my tears,
you've been my dearest friend,
and from the bottom of my heart, Nan,
my grateful thanks I send.

No matter what, you've always made
lots of time for me,
you make me feel so welcome
and as special as can be.

You've cheered me up so often
when I've been feeling down,
and you always
know exactly how
to chase away my frown.

For all these things and so much more
I'd really like to send
a great big loving 'thank you'
for being my most special friend.

Every step of the way, Nan,
you have guided me through life.
You've listened and you've understood
and you've given the best advice.

You have always helped me choose
the right path to take.
You've encouraged me to start again
and learn from my mistakes.

If there's one thing
I have learnt from you
it's to appreciate,
that the simple things
in life are the ones
that make it great.

You're the one who taught me, Nan,
to hold onto my dreams,
and to never stop believing
no matter how distant they may seem.

Through all the ups and downs of life
you've always helped me see,
that if I keep on trying
I'll be the best that I can be.

Of all the people in my life
you've always been the one,
who's shown an extra-special interest
in the things that I have done.

I hope you know, Nan, that it makes
my heart feel so glad,
to see how proud you've always been
of the successes I have had.

You've been there to congratulate
and to commiserate as well,
you've been the one who picked me up
every time I fell.

Nan you taught me lots of things
that I always keep in mind,
important things like honesty
and being considerate and kind.

Things like trying to understand
another's point of view,
and considering their feelings
before deciding what to say or do.

Nan, I've learned all of this first hand
just by watching you.
You've shown me by example
exactly what to do.

I'd see you, Nan, so often
doing favours, being kind,
always knowing the perfect words to say
to ease somebody's mind.

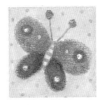

Nan you have the special gift
of making other people's day,
just by showing how much you care
with the things you do and say.

Putting others first, Nan,
comes naturally to you,
you have the warmest, biggest heart
and it shows in all you do.

Nan we have a special bond
that will last our whole lives through,
a bond that will never be broken
but will remain forever true.

Nan you're always in my heart
and that's where you belong,
and your presence
there is certain
to stay forever strong...

...giving warmth and comfort
helping me through each day,
reminding me how much you care
even if you are far away.

I can't think of anyone
in this whole world, it's true
who deserves the best that life can bring
quite as much as you.

I just hope you know, Nan,
if you ever need me I'll be there,
because wherever I might go
you know I'll always care.

It makes me
really happy to know
that no matter how
much time goes by,

whatever life may
have in store
we'll still be
special friends,
you and I.

Thank you Nan for being the light
that always guides my way.
Thanks for bringing out the sunshine
and chasing my clouds away.

Most of all Nan thank you
for so much love and care,
and for all the wonderful memories
that you and I can share.

As you read this little book
I really hope you know,
that although I seldom say it, Nan,
I will always love you so.

A Heartwarmers™
Gift Book

WPL

Also available from Heartwarmers™

Thank you Mum

For a Special Friend

For my Sister

For You Mum

100 Reasons why I Love You

For my Husband

To a Good Friend

Believe in Yourself

I Love You Because...

For a Special Daughter

For a Special Mum